M B O E

Social Mindfulness

A guide to meditations from
Mindfulness-Based
Organisational Education

Mark Leonard

The meditations referred to
throughout are available from
meditations.mindfulnessconnected.com

Mindfulness
Connected

First published in the United Kingdom by
Mindfulness Connected LTD 2019

Set in 10/13.844 Palatino
Designed & typeset by
Mindfulness Connected LTD

Dedicated to
the memory of

Tenzin Choedak

with thanks to

Professor Richard Gombrich

for his support and encouragement
through the years

Contents

Acknowledgments   7

Prologue   11

Introduction   15
    The importance of relatedness   15
    Following the programme   18

Stopping and starting again with the three-step reset   21
    Neurotechnology   21
    The three-step reset practice   22

Building foundations of mindfulness with the bodyscan   25
    Slowing down   25
    Body-based feelings   26
    The nature of threat   27
    Developing a regular meditation practice   29
    Bodyscan meditation   30

Building focus and confidence with posture and breath   33
    Motivation   33
    Being specific   34
    Posture and breath meditation   35
        Working with posture   36
        Mindfulness of breathing   36

Releasing patterns held in the body with stretching and sitting   39
    Embodied imprints and old stories   39
    Stretching and sitting meditation   40

Understanding our social selves with mindfulness of feelings   43
    Mindless self   43
    Feelings and objects   44
    Group-mind   45
    Mindfulness of feelings meditation   47

Deepening mindfulness meditation with concentration and allowing the mind to wander   51
    Living in an uncertain world   51
    Concentration and allowing the mind to wander meditation   52

Epilogue   55
    The path of no return   55
    Enlightenment   57

Glossary   61

Figures

1. Social mindfulness   17
2. 144 ten-minute periods in 24 hours   32
3. Flowchart of mindfulness meditation   54
    3a. Flowchart of concentration meditation
    3b. Flowchart of open-monitoring meditation
4. Leadership mindfulness   59

Meditations

The meditations referred to throughout are available from
meditations.mindfulnessconnected.com

Acknowledgments

This booklet has evolved through discussions and learning in formal contexts with: Juliet Adams, Julian Baginni, Geoff Bamford, Thorsten Barnhofer, Trish Bartley, Jamie Bristow, Vidyamala Burch, Margaret Chapman-Clarke, Tenzin Choedack, Mike Clayton, Sam Clayton, Fiamma Crucioli, Chris Cullen, Saul Deason, Khammai Dhammasami, Steven Egan, Melanie Fennel, Dimitri Gavriloff, Richard Gombrich, Marina Grazier, Tenzin Gyatso, Anne Hackman, Sarah Hennelly, Chris Jack, Jayaraja, Mira Jempe, Jon Kabat-Zinn, Cathy-Mae Karelse, Bernadette Lax, Robin Leonard, Anita Lewis, Rachel Lilley, Felix Lim, Janet McInnes, Sarah Methven, Karma Lodrö, Simon O'Donoghue, John Peacock, Dick Polak, Nick Pole, Amaranatho Robey, Joshua Smith, Craig Stevens, Nicholas Stone, Christina Surawy, John Teasdale, Dmitri Tikhonov, Karma Wangyal, Jackie Watson, Simon Wickham-Smith, Mark Williams, Kitty Wheater, William Woolf and many people who have attended courses and workshops.

I wish to acknowledge Danny Penman's input, making a short format of Mindfulness-Based Cognitive Therapy accessible, in the book he co-authored with Mark Williams, Mindfulness: A Practical Guided to Finding Peace in a Frantic World. This book provided a platform on which an evidence-based approach could be developed with the support of pioneering workplace champions. Sean Gilgallon, Chris Ridge and Helen Wiseman made it possible to develop and test the 'Frantic World' programme for staff from CVS Vets across the country. Cornelia Blunt, Simran Minhas, David

Richardson made it possible to develop and test Mindfulness-Based Organisational Education for staff at the Royal Orthopaedic Hospital under trial conditions (Krusche, A., Jack, C.D., Blunt, C. et al. Mindfulness (2019). https://doi.org/10.1007/s12671-019-01121-x).

I wish to thank Adele Krusche and Chris Jack for their research work, Robin Leonard for designing this booklet and Paul Davies, Harpal Dhatt, Sandra Rachaman and Kylie Short for copy editing and editorial input.

Mark Leonard, 14th March 2019.

Prologue

Everything in society has meaning and purpose shaped by culture. This may be obvious to everyone or it may not. What is explicit is what makes things attractive or unattractive. What is implicit may be hidden because it has never been recognised, but what is hidden will always have some power to unconsciously control.

Religious beliefs are tangled up with our sense of identity. Meditation has arisen in different cultures, at different times for different reasons. A new form of Buddhist meditation, created for lay Buddhists during the colonial period in Burma migrated to the West, to become 'mindfulness'.

Clinical psychologists, John Teasdale, Zindel Segal and Mark Williams adapted John Kabat-Zinn's Mindfulness-Based Stress Reduction (MBSR), for managing chronic pain and stress of living with chronic illness, as a treatment to prevent depression, which they named Mindfulness-Based Cognitive Therapy (MBCT).

Danny Penman then collaborated with Mark Williams to write a self-help book, Mindfulness: A Practical Guide to Finding Peace in a Frantic World with shorter guided meditations. These courses all follow an eight-week format, first devised by John Kabat-Zin for MBSR. Mark Leonard, and Chris Cullen co-taught the first 'Frantic World' course to students in Oxford. Mark Leonard and Marina Grazier then developed a six-week version of this course for the workplace.

The University of Oxford provided a fertile environment in which ideas about mindfulness could be explored and then a centre from which it could be disseminated. The Oxford Mindfulness

Centre (OMC) sprung from Professor Richard Gombrich's initiative to develop Buddhist Studies and Professor Mark Williams' work in the Department of Psychiatry. Geoffrey Bamford, who was working with Richard Gombrich, and Professor Mark Williams negotiated an agreement with The Warneford Hospital and Marjorie Wallace, Chief Executive of the mental health charity, SANE, to give the OMC its first home in the Prince of Wales International Centre, which was situated on the grounds of the Warneford Hosptial. Mark Leonard was involved in early discussions and worked in management roles from 2008 to 2013, before co-founding the OMC spin-out, The Mindfulness Exchange, with Marina Grazier.

Changing conditions create new possibilities, however, the new can only build on the old. The vertebrate eye is an example of a design that has incorporated poor design features from its evolutionary precursors. Nerves from light-sensitive cells run across the surface of the retina and then create a blind spot where they join the optic nerve. If it were possible to design the eye from scratch, it would make sense to run nerves from light-sensitive cells behind the retina. In a similar way, mindfulness courses include certain design features for no other reason than the fact that they have been inherited from their precursors.

The structure of the Mindfulness-Based Organisational Education (MBOE) programme has evolved out of a sequence of developments. Like the 'Frantic World' course for the workplace, it is a six-week programme. The MBOE programme builds on tried and tested teaching methods but takes a further step in adapting and restructuring its precursors. The main sources of ideas, other than those that are common to cognitive psychology and modern mindfulness meditation, come from systems biology, evolutionary psychology and the physiology of the mind-body connection.

As mindfulness changes the way we relate to beliefs about ourselves and others, it has the power to rewrite the narratives that shape our lives. Collectively, these individual changes may have systemic effects, which result in organisational and social change. This is true of all forms of mindfulness.

Mindfulness meditation may amount to no more than a series of simple attentional exercises, however, its practice does not take place in a vacuum. The ideas we associate with it have a powerful effect on how we give meaning to the practice and the changes that result.

Therapeutic mindfulness programmes tend to present mindfulness as a value free intervention and allow participants on courses to make sense of its practice through a process of personal discovery. MBOE takes a different approach; one that is more profound than managing stress. It is designed to develop understanding that empowers and leads to systemic change through intentional activity in groups as well as on an individual basis.

Introduction

The importance of relatedness

Mindfulness has become a household word, but it means many different things to different people. The commonly held view is that it reduces stress, anxiety and depression. In organisations and on a policy level, it is seen as a cost-effective means of improving mental wellbeing or reducing mental ill health. With increasing levels of mental health problems, more and more people are learning about it.

MBOE is a new 'social mindfulness' programme that combines mindfulness practice with a sense of human relatedness. This changes the way mindfulness is taught and practiced to make it a force for organisational and social change. It is designed to develop insight into the way we create a sense of separate self and how this creates subconscious biases. It helps people understand their motives, communicate effectively and cooperate in times of change.

The human mind evolved to function in a safe social environment. Social Baseline Theory (SBT) explains how the sense of safety produced by the group is advantageous because it satisfies laws of the efficient use of energy in an ecosystem. The group creates a social baseline of safety that reduces energy needed by individuals to be vigilant to threat from enemies or predators.

Modern living creates a separate sense of self and this causes stress. As self-help or therapy, mindfulness reduces the stress caused by this separate sense of self. Similarly, MBOE reduces stress, however, it recognises that stress is a natural reaction to modern life and empowers people to act constructively to bring about change.

On an individual basis, **mindfulness meditation involves a series of simple attentional procedures that interrupt the internal narrative and increase awareness of body-based feelings.** On an individual basis, mindfulness practice reduces over-active thinking and reconnects body and mind. When mindfulness is understood as a social process, it releases the power of the most highly evolved social mind in nature to find new ways of navigating change.

Stories give us meaning but they also control what we think and how we act. We act out our personal stories in a bigger story that defines identity. Stories tell us what to expect and what we must do. They tell us who is powerful and who we may ignore. They tell us who we can trust and who we cannot.

If we believe mindfulness practice is a self-help tool that enables us to function better, we are likely to be motivated to practice it for individualistic reasons. This can even become a strategy for denial and avoidance. On an organisational level, it may become a means to maintain compliant behaviour or even social control in wider society.

MBOE is an evidence-based programme originally developed from MBCT. MBCT treats the human mind as an individual system of neurological, psychological and behavioural processes. From this perspective, some individuals are more vulnerable to stress than others and mindfulness helps some people who experience mental health problems to function as productive members of society.

By contrast, MBOE applies mindfulness to help understand the way we imagine ourselves and others, and how this makes us feel and act. Not only does this give us the power to rewrite the narratives that define us personally, it becomes a social process that influences the way we communicate, cooperate and organise ourselves. Understanding social mindfulness gives us the power to become agents of change.

As well as reducing stress and increasing mindfulness, MBOE improves Basic Psychological Needs at Work Scale, which is a measure of intrinsic motivation. There are three elements to this measure: autonomy, competence and relatedness. Figure 1 places these subjective perceptions in a dynamic scheme, with behaviour fostered by social mindfulness, to create resilient culture.

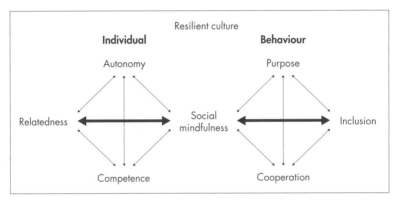

Figure 1. Social mindfulness

Many people find it is helpful to learn to meditate in a group because this reduces the sense of social threat that creates stress. A sense of social safety and individual mindfulness practice act together to create a sense of connection in the group and a shared sense of identity.

The MBOE programme structure builds learning on group activities. Those who join the programme learn about how we create a separate sense of self when we feel a sense of threat and how this sense of self changes when we make connections with others. This makes MBOE not only an advanced approach to teaching mindfulness meditation, it is also a powerful tool to create social cohesion in organisations and communities.

Our sense of relatedness with others is fundamentally important to us as social beings. Often, we do not understand that the very root of our suffering and the suffering we cause others, is the disconnection we experience in our lives.

If we are struggling, we feel isolated and unable to ask for support. In other situations, we feel uniquely privileged to indulge our wants. These patterns of behaviour leave a trail of destruction behind them and, in the end, we become victims of our own devices.

For those who suffer from self-critical thinking, mindfulness will not help much without a sense that we are all human and we are not alone in our failings. When mindfulness practice is about living in the moment without consideration of others, it can become self-serving or even nihilistic. Mindfulness practice must be built on a foundation of relatedness if it is to have positive outcomes.

Motivation in therapy is based on the desire to be free from suffering and perhaps to function better in society. Little is explained in MBCT and this can lead to a vale of mystery that may be exploited by the therapist. In place of explanation, therapeutic mindfulness courses derived from MBSR believe the teacher's embodiment of their mindfulness practice plays an important role. By contrast MBOE is a clearly structured course that supports incremental learning by exploiting the potential for affecting experience through social interactions in the class as well as with theory and personal practice. This creates a sense of autonomy, as opposed to dependence on the therapist/teacher by clearly explaining the what, why and how of social mindfulness.

Following the programme

MBOE is a six-week programme that covers all you need to know about mindfulness meditation. The programme is designed for those who have no experience of mindfulness meditation. Experienced meditators who participate in the programme gain new insights that enables them to deepen their practice and engage in working life with a greater sense of purpose.

There is a new guided meditation each week, which is introduced in the class and practiced during the week. Each of the following chapters review learning presented in weekly classes and supports self-study during the week.

The learning in class is built around group activities. These activities also create a sense of connection with others participating in the programme. This cultivate relatedness, which then provides a sound platform on which to develop a mindfulness meditation practice. The group then follows guided mindfulness meditations in class before practicing independently during the week.

This booklet may also be used as a self-study guide. On a self-study basis you can cultivate relatedness simply by **recollecting connections**. Start with friends and family, then work colleagues and anyone else you know. Include as many people as you can think of that you see from time to time. Recollect something about each person as you bring them to mind. Follow this practice every day for the first four weeks of the course.

Stopping and starting again with the three-step reset

Neurotechnology

Technological innovation increases resources available to society. Society, human experience and the way we see ourselves changes as a result. The information revolution operates in an attentional marketplace. Competing demands for attention and the pressure of modern lifestyles drive disconnection and stress.

Unlike the silicon-based information processing systems, there is no clear difference between hardware and software in the living human brain. It is made up of billions of living cells and changes with every bit of information it processes. The brain processes information physiologically: synapses fire, networks of connections adapt to patterns of experience, brain cells are born, live and die.

The challenges of modern living drive problem-solving thinking that comes with an implicit sense of something that needs to be done to make us feel safe and content. Problems arise when an implicit sense of threat triggers a low-level fight or flight reaction. We need strategies to stop ourselves running around and around in circles exhausting ourselves while endlessly recreating the conditions that cause stress.

The Default Mode Network (DMN) of the brain processes higher cognitive functions of the human mind, however, the conditions we experience today are very different to those in which we evolved. We are bombarded by information. We feel constantly judged by our ability to solve problems. We believe we are separate individuals who are responsible for ourselves alone. We often live lonely lives disconnected from a sense of community. The emotional disruption and overstimulation we experience results in DMN overactivity. This overactivity is associated with mental ill health, disrupts our ability to think around problems and damages our ability to build supportive relationships.

On the other hand, the ability to disengage the DMN when we focus attention is associated with a range of improved higher cognitive functions, including social and emotional skills. In effect, mindfulness practice enables us to manage maladapted stressful responses to modern life by developing our ability to interrupt the activity of this network.

We need to start by recognising the needs of the human nervous system, which was evolved to meet the demands of life in very different social conditions, and work with them. First, we need to stop, before we can take stock and examine the ideas that shape our lives.

The three-step reset practice

The **three-step reset** involves:

1. stopping for a few moments,
2. acknowledging what is going on in the mind, and
3. noticing what is going on in the body.

The benefits of mindfulness practice come from training attention, reducing mental activity driven by stress and reconnecting the mind with feelings in the body. The main objective of the **three-step reset** is to develop a habit of stopping and noticing what is going on.

The **three-step reset** is a short, structured mindfulness exercise that we can use to stop for a moment and disengage attention from the internal narrative to give the nervous system a rest. It has three distinct stages, which introduce some key themes in mindfulness practice: self-awareness and self-acceptance, focusing attention on sensations of breathing to reduce mental activity and grounding awareness in the body.

Building foundations of mindfulness with the bodyscan

Slowing down

When there is not much going on in our experience, we look for something that will entertain us or occupy the mind. When we do not have something to do, the mind fills the space with story-telling, solving problems in our imagination and day-dreaming.

When there are underlying patterns of threat or stress, the human mind produces a story based around a separate sense of self; what it is that we need and what we have to do to get it. This separate sense of self is interested in survival and often sees identity, status and power as the means to get what we need.

With patterns of thinking free from a sense of threat, the mind is not preoccupied with the internal commentary of self-criticism, blame and problem solving. Then, digestion, cellular renewal and tissue repair take place, and the higher cognitive functions of the mind come up with intuitions and useful insights.

When we feel safe and the mind slows down, the body rests and we become more aware of how we feel. There may be pleasant feelings, but sometimes we become more aware of uncomfortable feelings, for example, discomfort caused by inflammation or stiffness. (We learn more about how mindfulness practice helps to reduce physical pain in the **stretching and sitting** meditation.)

Body-based feelings

When we think of the senses we think of 'the five senses': touch, smell, taste, sight and hearing, but we do not actually have a commonly used word for the sense organ of the body itself. This is remarkable because body-based feelings are not just the emotional glue in our intimate lives, they give meaning to everything we think, say and do. This sense organ of the body is made of billions of nerve endings, embedded in the muscles, joints and connective tissue, including the skin. These nerve endings are sensitive to pain, temperature, stretch, pressure and vibration.

The physiological terms that refer to these senses are: somatosensory perception (feelings in muscles, connective tissue and skin), proprioception (posture and movement) and interoception (feelings in the visceral organs of the belly and chest, including heart, gut and lungs). Much of the time we are completely unaware of these feelings until we injure ourselves and experience pain or when we are having sex.

When we are stressed and disconnected from our feelings, we do things to 'get out of our mind'. We seek pleasure and avoid uncomfortable feelings. This often involves substance misuse and social activities that enable us to lose a sense of a separate self. Extreme sports and exercise have similar effects. These activities may become addictive because doing things that numb uncomfortable feelings also cut us off from feelings of pleasure and contentment.

Like all mindfulness meditation practices, the **bodyscan** requires some effort at first. Unlike activities that stimulate the senses more intensively, the **bodyscan** trains the nervous system to be more sensitive to feelings in the body.

At first, we may become more aware of uncomfortable feelings that are normally masked by mental activity. It is important to persevere with the **bodyscan**, as these feelings will fade as the nervous system adjusts.

Without becoming more sensitive to body-based feelings, the mind will continue to seek distraction. It will be hard to make progress without developing this body-based awareness. With practice, the **bodyscan** will make us feel more alive.

The nature of threat

When we experience some kind of threat, the brain prepares the body to escape or protect itself. The bodily functions of digestion, growth and tissue repair shut down when the endocrine system (glands which produce hormones) releases 'fight or flight' hormones into the blood-stream. Breathing rate increases and the heart pumps blood to the muscles to enable the body to act fast. Attention is focused on the source of threat and the course of action needed to evade or neutralise it.

The fight or flight reaction triggers automatic responses. There is no need to be aware of feelings in the body unless they are needed to deal with the immediate threat. There is no time for curiosity, learning about new things, being open to new possibilities or connecting with others.

Two weeks after an incident of acute stress, there is an increase in the rate of production of new brain cells in rats. This may indicate that the body and brain are designed to process the emotional after-effects of traumatic experience and then learn from the experience some time after the threat has passed. For humans, however, recovery from stress and trauma is not just a neurological process, it is a social process that results in a new sense of identity and purpose. If we do not have access to rituals or healing rites that enable us to do this, we are likely to suffer serious negative effects.

In nature, dangerous encounters with predators, enemies or deadly poisonous animals would happen sporadically. These events are unpredictable, short-lived incidents. The experience of threat is very different in life today; we rarely experience threat to life or limb. We spend our lives focusing our efforts on managing predictable problems and challenges from which we are rarely free. We always have some goal in sight and when we achieve it, we seek another to give our efforts meaning. We are addicted to an endless cycle of striving and the excitement we get from success.

We are rewarded for solving problems and our sense of self-worth becomes fused with our ability to achieve goals. When we are successful, we feel good but there is a cost. The sense of threat we experience today is more to do with our sense of self-worth than real or immediate physical danger. Just like a real threat to life and limb, this reduces our sensitivity to feelings. We never escape from ourselves and never really feel content. We never really feel safe and can never truly rest.

The human mind interprets the threat of failure as a physical threat to life and limb rather than just a threat to our imagined sense of self. If we are caught up in striving to achieve, we are running on adrenalin of excitement and pressure. The body never gets a chance to rest and repair. This causes stiffness and tension in the body and the nervous system becomes exhausted. This does not just have a negative effect on well-being and our ability to think clearly, it cuts us off from our feelings and interferes with our ability to enjoy things that nourish us emotionally.

If we fail, we may feel inadequate and drive ourselves to succeed. If we believe we are responsible for improving our lives and do not have the resources or opportunity to progress, we believe we are inadequate. If we cannot accept that our feelings are a natural response to social conditions, we may try to analyse what is wrong and come to the conclusion that something is not right with us. We blame ourselves. This produces a spiral of stress, which steals our energy and interferes with our ability to think creatively and connect with others. It strangles the very feelings of well-being and pleasure that renew our energy and we become depressed.

Developing a regular meditation practice

Embodied patterns of stress and trauma involve physiological and neurological processes. Animals have evolved trauma-release behaviour, however, humans need to release stress and trauma socially. In traditional societies, rituals perform this function. Rituals renew individual and group identity, creating a social space where people can share, witness and process emotional pain.

Today, the traditional stories that enabled us to come together to perform these functions have lost their power and so we invent new ways of doing this. Mindfulness meditation represents one method of satisfying this need. It makes sense to us because we can understand how it works in scientific, rather than mythological terms.

Many people often find that the social process of meditating in a group supports their practice. This comes from setting a time to meet, peer support and the sense of safety that comes from being part of a group. In an organisation or community, meditating together creates social connections, shared values and a reservoir of resilience that comes from the sense of collective identity that would otherwise have been produced by a traditional ritual.

Whenever we are learning a new skill, it is best to take one step at a time and set up conditions that help us to learn. It is important to feel comfortable when we start to practice mindfulness meditation. At least to start with, we really need to feel we will not be disturbed. It is a good idea to set aside a time and create a space, which we can dedicate to our personal practice.

Figure 2 represents 24 hours split up into 144 sections. If you spend eight hours asleep, this leaves 96 ten-minute periods. If you spend eight hours at work this leaves 64 ten-minute periods. All MBOE meditations are ten minutes long (apart from the **three-step reset** and **recollecting connections**). If you reserve one ten-minute period for meditating, there will be 63 left. It makes it easier to establish any new habit by establishing a routine. It will help to develop a meditation practice by reserving the same ten-minute period to follow a guided meditation each day.

Bodyscan meditation

The **bodyscan** involves:

1. focusing attention on specific parts of the body;
2. directing attention from one part of the body to the next;
3. noticing the raw qualities of sensations that are present, or perhaps noticing that there are no sensations that can be perceived, in different parts of the body; and
4. noticing thoughts come into the mind, perhaps thinking about sensations or absence of sensations, then returning the focus of attention back to noticing the raw qualities of sensations that are present.

When we are deprived of levels of stimulation that we are used to, we get bored and distracted, or feel lonely. This triggers a sense of unease. We find it hard to be content and it takes us some time to relax and reconnect with feelings in the body.

Like all mindfulness meditation practices, the **bodyscan** involves paying attention to sensations. This interrupts patterns of positive feedback between thinking and emotions, however, the **bodyscan** also develops awareness of feelings in the body. These are the feelings we have when we are enjoying nourishing activities and relationships.

Becoming conscious of feelings in the body makes it possible to know when they change with different thoughts and emotions and this makes it possible to notice when our attention wanders. Feelings of discomfort trigger a reaction to do something to make us feel comfortable. Being more consciously aware of feelings before we react gives us the chance to think before we act.

The fact is, as a human being, we are going to have some kind of pattern of thinking and a sense of 'who we are' that is going to be imprinted on patterns of tension, stiffness and feelings (or disconnection from them) in the body. The **bodyscan** trains the nervous system to reconnect with feelings while learning to control attention. It can take years of practice to learn to feel safe and at ease in the body without some kind of distraction. This can be to do with past traumatic experience or just years of pressure to achieve goals, attempting to be perfect or trying to feel 'good enough'.

When attention wanders, this is often because we are bored. We want stimulation. We want things to feel better than the way they feel to us in the present moment. We can easily get caught up in a pattern of constantly monitoring the discrepancy between current conditions and how we would prefer things to be. This can easily become a constant state of anxiousness.

When the mind wanders, it is important to continue following the instructions as that is what will bring results. This training of our attention is teaching the mind to be less vigilant to minor discomfort and reduces over-active patterns of discrepancy monitoring. This reduces our sensitivity to discomfort and increases our ability to enjoy pleasant feelings when we have them.

In the end, it is the understanding that we gain from seeing how the mind works, as well as the physiological, neurological and emotional effects of mindfulness practice, that improves quality of life. The power of mindfulness meditation is that it produces an embodied shift in perception and a deeper understanding of what makes us who we are in relationship with others. The foundation of mindfulness meditation involves reducing activity in the mind by focusing attention on sensations and developing awareness of feelings in the body, which is exactly what the **bodyscan** does.

If you find the **bodyscan,** or any of the mindfulness meditations in this course too difficult, just do as much of it as you can comfortably and see if you can do a little more each day. It is very important not to create more tension by trying too hard to practice mindfulness meditation. Results will come from crossing backwards and forwards over the threshold of comfort and discomfort; exploring the uncomfortable and then returning to take refuge in a place of safety and comfort. Like anything, we need a combination of confidence and a challenge to learn and that is just the same with mindfulness meditation.

10×144

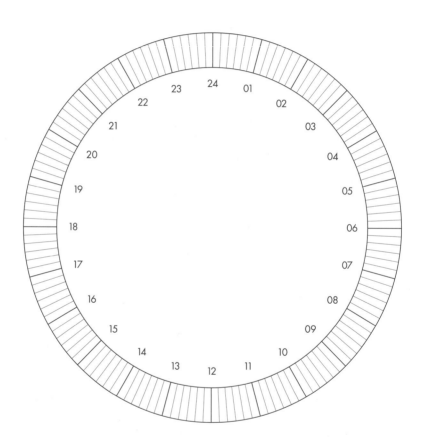

Figure 2. 144 ten-minute periods in 24 hours

**Building focus and confidence
with posture and breath**

Motivation

M otivation is important. Motivation to practice mindfulness meditation may vary. In the end, what is common to everyone is the desire to live a happy and fulfilling life. Mindfulness meditation helps us to see that a narrow sense of self-interest is an illusion and our happiness is inseparable from that of others. This enables us to discover a deeper sense of purpose that is the energy that sustains us.

Sometimes, people come to the decision that mindfulness meditation is not for them. Something about it may feel uncomfortable. Instructions and explanations may be unclear, or mindfulness meditations may be too long. Often, it is just because it is hard to establish new habits even if we know they are good for us.

These meditations and the MBOE programme are designed to make developing mindfulness in busy working lives as easy to integrate and sustain as possible. Group work in class is intended to create a sense of support and encouragement by connecting with others. The programme empowers by clearly explaining the what, why and how and offers short meditations that can fit into even the busiest of days. This course, however, still may not work for everyone.

Whatever it is we are doing, we must learn to acknowledge things as they are if we are going to make progress. The same is true for mindfulness meditation practice – its power comes, not just from the way it trains us to maintain attention, regulate emotions and develop awareness, but also from developing self-acceptance. This comes from bringing an attitude of acceptance to the patterns of thoughts, emotions and sensations we become aware of with mindfulness practice. Accepting ourselves and others as they are gives us the resources to listen, be compassionate and have the patience and resilience to make progress, one step at a time.

Comparing experience with expectations about how it should be, is counterproductive in mindfulness meditation in exactly the same way as it is counterproductive in daily life. One of the most important skills learnt in mindfulness meditation is how to regulate the part of the mind that evaluates what is going on from moment to moment. We may be pleased with how our meditation is going. Sooner or later a time will come when we feel it is not going so well. We may then become disappointed that mindfulness is not producing the results we expect.

Growth, by its very nature, is uncomfortable at times and until we encounter uncomfortable feelings in mindfulness meditation, nothing much will change. It is easy to lose motivation at the very point an opportunity for growth is being presented to us.

Being specific

Understanding how the mind constructs what we believe to be true helps us to challenge our assumption. Mindfulness helps us to disentangle our emotional reactions from our thoughts. It helps us to be more comfortable with uncertainty, reduce biased ways of seeing things and be open to new possibilities.

What we discover may surprise us, however, the way we feel and respond will depend on how we identify with our beliefs. Some new ideas produce positive feelings. We may also feel uncomfortable when our beliefs are challenged. As mindfulness practice helps us to disentangle our feelings from facts this enables us to process emotions and become more resilient as we adapt to new realities that come with change.

Learning to be specific about what we observe enables us to counteract our tendency to overgeneralise, however, we cannot recollect what we notice unless we pay attention to what is going on in experience. As mindfulness entails noticing what is going on in the present moment, mindfulness and recollecting specific details of what we observe are mutually supportive skills.

Putting what we have noticed into words and describing it to another person, who is listening attentively is part of the learning experience. This helps to build a sense of connection and feel less defensive.

These skills become useful in all kinds of areas in our lives. They help us to actively listen to others and share information that is uncomfortable to hear, in a constructive way.

Posture and breath meditation

The **posture and breath** meditation involves:

1. maintaining an upright and awake posture;
2. focusing attention on sensations of breathing; and
3. when attention is distracted, checking posture and returning attention to sensations of breathing.

Mindfulness of **posture and breath** becomes more than a means to settle the mind. When we can accept that the mind will wander over and over again, we discover that the mind settles more easily. This helps us to learn to let go of self-critical thinking and be more accepting of ourselves and others.

Working with posture

Body-language signals to others how we feel about ourselves and in turn informs how others relate to us. Posture also affects mood, thinking and self-image. Sitting with good posture tells the brain via the central nervous system (transmitting signals from the network of nerve endings in the connective tissue, joints and muscles that detect stretch and pressure – proprioception), that we feel confident and less concerned about what others think about us. Simply holding an upright posture improves mood and reduces stressful or anxious thinking. This is why it is important to sit upright in sitting meditation.

Sedentary lifestyles and stress often result in poor posture. This feeds low mood as well as being a cause of chronic back-pain. Changing habits takes time and to start with, it can be difficult to hold an upright posture for long. Too much effort can lead to stiffness and tension, which may cause more problems if we persist.

Start sitting upright, using the minimum of muscular effort. When the posture slumps, it is just a question of making small adjustments to sit upright again. The task is to just do this over and over again. This does not mean that we should hold this posture all day long, however, most of us do need to become more aware of our posture and get into the habit of adjusting it from time to time. Like most skills, progress will be made one step at a time with patience and awareness. Just sitting becomes a mindfulness meditation in itself.

Mindfulness of breathing

In mindfulness of breathing, we focus attention on sensations of breathing and when we notice that attention has become absorbed in thinking, just returning attention to focus on sensations of breathing again. We still have an idea of what we want to happen: paying attention to the posture and focusing attention on sensations of breathing. Monitoring the movements of attention. We have to pay attention, to notice when the mind is distracted by thoughts and return attention to **posture and breath,** over and over again. This develops focus and our ability to act with intention.

When what is uncomfortable does come up, letting go of expectations and returning to the simple steps in mindfulness meditation creates the space for real progress to take place. As always, the process in mindfulness meditation is very simple, but there are many distractions. Over and over again, the mind will wander and, over and over again, the task in the **posture and breath** meditation is simply to disengage attention from thinking about what is going on, renew effort to maintaining an upright posture and focus attention on sensations of breathing.

With practice, focusing on sensations of breathing has a calming effect, however, it is quite common for people to find that this produces some anxiety and increased mental activity at first. As always, the key to making progress is just noticing what is taking place. If uncomfortable feelings become distressing, just stop or focus attention on other sensations e.g. sensations of pressure on the soles of the feet or just pay attention to maintaining an upright posture for the duration of the meditation.

The vagus nerve informs the central nervous system about the physiological state of the visceral organs – stomach, intestines, heart and lungs. These are feelings in the body, like 'butterflies' in the belly, that we are often not aware of. The body breathes automatically but we can also control the breath consciously. At first it can feel strange to focus on sensations of breathing. This not just because this makes us more aware of our emotional state but because focussing on the breath changes patterns of breathing and so changes our emotional state.

Vagal tone is a measure of overall wellbeing and physiological resilience. It is a measure of the rhythmic variation of heart rate synchronised with breathing in and out. Poor vagal tone is an indication of chronic stress. There is a calming effect on the out-breath (parasympathetic activation) and the heart rate slows. There is an opposite physiological effect on the in-breath (sympathetic activation) and the heart rate increases slightly. The sequence of paying attention to different parts of the cycle of breathing in the **posture and breath** meditation naturally produces slightly longer out-breaths than in-breaths, reducing the overall heart rate, which has a calming effect. This 'entrains' the rhythms of variations in the heart rate with the breath, improving vagal tone.

**Releasing patterns held in the body
with stretching and sitting**

Embodied imprints and old stories

As a human being, we have an idea of who we are. We create a sense of identity out of patterns of thoughts, feelings and things we do. When our sense of identity is threatened, we feel uncomfortable and we rationalise our feelings by replaying old stories that justify the way we feel.

The moment we react, reason becomes an afterthought. We think we are in control of our actions, but this is an illusion. Slowing things down in mindfulness meditation enables us to learn to recognise how these automatic patterns arise. When we get to know these patterns, we have a choice. We can feed a pattern with the energy of attention or we can starve it by disengaging attention from the story and then neutralise it by processing body-based feelings with awareness.

As well as shaping the structure of the brain, patterns of thinking, mood, posture and movement become physiologically imprinted on the body. Mindfulness meditation is an intentional way of doing nothing consciously, which not only helps us to become aware of these patterns, it allows physiological processes to repair tissue affected by posture and stress. Mindfulness meditation processes these embodied imprints. It neurologically integrates renewal and realignment taking place in the body.

In fact, doing nothing intentionally with awareness is not actually doing nothing at all – it is watching and listening. It informs the physiological systems of the body that there is no immediate threat and so no need to trigger a fight or flight reaction. This does not just help us to be less reactive in difficult situations, it helps us to stay calm and keep a clear head. It keeps our perception open to new sensory information. It helps us notice specific details that give us a more realistic picture of what is going on. It helps us to let go of old stories and move on.

Remaining present with awareness enables us to listen to what others are trying to say rather than always trying to fix things. This tells others that we do not feel that there is any need to be alarmed at what may concern them. It tells them that they are safe saying whatever it is they have to say. It makes it possible for people to share observations and thoughts that might otherwise remain unspoken. It helps us to be open and brings people together. It gives a group the information it will need to adapt to changing conditions.

Just like the individual mind, the social mind works adaptively in a state that is free from threat. In this state, there is no sense of uncertainty and no need for answers. Exploration and play replace the perception of problems and the need for solutions.

Stretching and sitting meditation

The **stretching and sitting** meditation involves:

1. exploring sensations of stretching;
2. noticing discomfort in the body that comes from holding an upright posture;
3. exploring the sensations of discomfort; and
4. noticing the urge to move and moving consciously.

The thin sheets of connective tissue that hold tissues and organs in their place (fascia) do not stretch much. It is the way we respond to uncomfortable sensations that causes us to tense up and this is what restricts movement. When we are curious about sensations of stretching, muscles relax enabling more movement and this makes it possible for layers of fascia to slide over each other. This improves the flow of lymph through the mesh-like structure of collagen fibres that make up the layers of fascia. This removes waste products of metabolism from the muscles and so reduces tension allowing greater movement and reducing stiffness in the joints.

By improving movement and releasing tension in the body, we are releasing the long-term imprint of patterns of thinking, mood, movement, posture and behaviour on physiology. It is not just improved flexibility and reduced muscle tension that enables us to sit comfortably for longer. It becomes easier to settle the mind in meditation because stretching with awareness is also releasing the embodied patterns that feed judgmental, threat-related reactions and overactive problem-solving patterns of thinking.

When we sit still, upright and awake for a few minutes, attention gets drawn to places in the body where sensations of tension or pressure build up. Mindfulness of sitting involves noticing how these sensations appear in awareness and then noticing the way feelings of discomfort are produced in the mind. We want the discomfort to go away and we want to move or stretch.

This gives us the opportunity to see how all sorts of sensations and patterns of thoughts and feelings come and go. Simply observing thoughts and emotions gives us some perspective and helps us to be less reactive.

Feelings of discomfort arise as a secondary reaction to raw sensations. Becoming aware of uncomfortable feelings in the body in mindfulness meditation gives us the opportunity to explore them before reacting to them. We can then become aware of the way we may be tensing up as a natural response to avoiding pain.

The uncomfortable feelings that we become aware of in mindfulness meditation are at least partly produced by imprints of patterns of posture and mood on our physiology that reflect the way we see ourselves. The responses we have to uncomfortable feelings will, similarly, reflect patterns of reactivity to uncomfortable feelings we experience in social situations.

We discover that when we want pain to go away, we create a sense of self that is wanting the pain to stop, and conversely, often the pain gets worse. We discover that when we explore the raw qualities of sensations, the sense of self that wants the pain to stop disappears and the sense of discomfort becomes less intense.

The same is true of uncomfortable feelings that come when we imagine a sense of self that has a problem. When we focus attention on these feelings, we find that the sense of self and the problem, become less real. This skill becomes useful in all kinds of situations in life e.g. when we feel nervous in social situations.

Exploring what we find uncomfortable becomes one of the most important lessons of mindfulness meditation because it shifts the way we relate to discomfort from avoidance, resistance or denial, to curiosity. This is a shift from an automatic avoidance response to an approach response. This dials down the discomfort produced by wanting the discomfort to stop and releases tension that sustains it. Then discomfort becomes a rich source of information. The brain processes what is going on, reducing the perception of pain. Tissue repair can take place and nervous connections change. The mind produces insights about ourselves, our beliefs and the way we relate to others.

There is, however, a fine balance between using effort to continue with the practice of exploring what is going on and managing the experience of pain. The practice asks us to train the mind and be patient and kind to the body at the same time. There is a point when it is just time to move to ease the discomfort. Noticing how this all happens gives us insight into the way discomfort in the body builds when we want it to go away. Slowing things down gives us the opportunity to respond to the stimulus and move or stretch to ease the discomfort with conscious intention, as opposed to reacting automatically to sensory triggers. This gives us an opportunity to learn to act with free will as opposed to reacting to uncomfortable feelings automatically.

Understanding our social selves
with mindfulness of feelings

Mindless self

When a stick falls out of a tree and hits you on the head, it would be senseless to get angry with the tree because the tree and the stick do not intend to cause you harm. It is just a random event. If our emotional reactions are automatic processes, why then do we get angry when someone throws a stick at us? We get angry because we imagine a person who intends to cause us harm and we imagine ourselves as the target of their harmful intent.

We can only choose not to react when we become consciously aware of how our thoughts, sense of self and how our feelings are automatically constructed. This is the power of mindfulness: it gives us the agency we thought we had by seeing that we never had it in the first place. It helps us to gain wisdom that comes from realising that much of human behaviour is merely produced by mindless, automatic reactions. While we may be responsible for our actions, this insight helps us to realise that the suffering we experience is blameless.

We can feel sadness and compassion when we stop criticising our imaginary selves or blaming the imaginary person who has caused us harm. Then we may gain the energy and resilience that comes from a purposeful life without the drain of destructive emotions.

Our social environment is a complex dynamic of shared beliefs, the way we organise ourselves and the way we distribute resources. If each of us can work to our strengths and can adapt what we do to fit the needs of the group, the group can achieve much more than the sum of individual efforts. This can change patterns of resource use and make group activity more efficient and productive. To work together we have to let go of a sense of ourselves as separate individuals, focus on collective goals and identify with the common good of the group.

Feelings and objects

The human mind evolved to understand what is going on in the minds of those around us and make sense of everything through stories. Our ability to imagine stories gave us the power to see cause and effect at work in the world around us. We learnt to see problems and to solve them, however, treating uncomfortable feelings as problems is the cause of much psychological ill health. We need to accept our feelings and only apply problem-solving skills to objects and situations. Mindfulness gives us the ability to see the difference between feelings and objects and apply different strategies that work in these two different worlds.

This power of imagining what is going on in another's mind also gives us the power to imagine what is going on in our own mind. We can imagine ourselves thinking thoughts and feeling emotions. This also gives us the power to imagine ourselves differently, but growth takes sleight of hand because wanting to change ourselves can easily turn into a self-critical voice. We have to be understanding, kind and patient with our imaginary selves in the same way that we have to be understanding, kind and patient with others, if we want to give them the opportunity to grow.

Becoming more aware of how we feel is the first step, but nothing much changes until we are able to accept how we feel. It is only when we can accept ourselves, imperfect as we are, that we can begin to loosen patterns of self-criticism and blame that feed negative emotions and destructive beliefs about ourselves and others.

By acknowledging our feelings, we create a sense of safety that would otherwise be produced by being acknowledged and heard by others. Feeling safe when we bring to mind a memory that comes with strong emotions enables us to accept the feelings we have and be curious about them. Feeling safe and focusing attention on sensations of feelings in the body creates a new and less potent memory of the painful experience we have brought to mind. This reduces its power to trigger reactions.

When old memories lose their power to trigger reactions, we are more able to see things differently and learn from them. We learn to replace self-critical thinking and blame with understanding. The narrative of a separate self loses its power over us. Sorrow and sadness replace painful feelings and we respond to suffering with compassion.

As we learn to process painful narratives and emotions with mindfulness, we learn new strategies to manage difficult situations. When we change our behaviour, this changes the way others respond to us and so affects the whole emotional and behavioural dynamics of situations.

Group-mind

We naturally work together to defend or promote our collective interests. We create a sense of collective identity built around shared beliefs and resources. We recognise others who are like us. We fuse facts with stories and stories with identity. When facts challenge our beliefs, we ignore them or deny them.

When we are confronted with uncertainty, we feel threatened and stereotypes tell us who is on our side and who is not. If we do not work to build connections with those we see as different to ourselves, stereotypes become signals that undermine trust and give us permission to exclude, dehumanise and abuse.

Mindfulness helps us to down-regulate emotional reactions and make us aware of how we create a story to protect ourselves when changing situations challenge our beliefs or threaten our interests. It helps us to notice how our biased perceptions stop us from noticing what is actually going on. It helps us to separate facts from feelings and consider the facts on their own merit while accepting the way we (and others) feel. It helps us to make better informed decisions and build a more inclusive sense of identity in times of change.

In modern society we need to believe we are responsible for our own self-improvement and that we should be rightly rewarded for our personal achievements. Those who do not have the resources to succeed, however, feel unfairly treated, which has a destructive effect on their willingness to work for collective goals. Low motivation feeds a downward spiral of self-sabotage, failure to achieve and resentment. While we may never be able to create a utopian society, we do have to manage the social fallout of inequality because, when it is perceived as injustice, it has a damaging effect on social cohesion and group identity.

If we avoid difficult feelings, we end up repressing them. We cut ourselves off from our feelings and get trapped in reactive patterns of thinking and acting. Over time, these patterns lead to stress, depression and/or anxiety. If we only listen to the voices of those who confirm our sense of identity and ignore messengers who come with uncomfortable news, we will miss information that will help us grow and adapt to change.

The individual mind functions very much like the mind of a group. To feel included, people need to be able to express themselves without threat of rejection. They need to feel that their contribution is valued by others. If a group (or society) is not able to listen to a dissenting voice, some will repress their feelings and suffer as a result. Some get stuck in destructive roles. Some just move on and the group (or society) loses the diversity of voice that enables it to adapt to change.

The most powerful and sustainable form of motivation is the intrinsic reward felt from making a meaningful contribution to those we identify with. A sense of social purpose and the power to make a meaningful contribution transforms the stress of striving into a source of resilience and energy.

Who we are is constantly changing in different social contexts. As we change, our relationships change. Sometimes we long for change. At other times we resist change. Mindfulness practice helps us to be more aware of change as it happens, accept what is going on and adapt.

Becoming aware of how the mind works, not only helps us to understand ourselves and others better, it enables us to see the way group–mind works. Maintaining a low level of emotional reactivity sets up a similar response in others, allowing the group to reconcile differences and transform patterns of destructive emotions into a productive force.

As this group behaviour becomes established, discussions become a creative exercise instead of a game of strategy and power. Those who are less confident feel safe and more able to contribute. The group-mind becomes an integrated system that coordinates the activity of individuals. The group becomes dynamic, resilient and adaptive.

Mindfulness of feelings meditation

The **mindfulness of feelings** meditation involves:

1. visualising situations with different people;
2. exploring thoughts and feelings that arise in different situations;
3. becoming more familiar with thoughts and feelings; and
4. accepting thoughts and feelings as they are.

Mindfulness meditation helps us to regulate our emotions by being aware of them and gives us a window to see the mind creating the imaginary world of our experience. The **mindfulness of feelings** meditation gives us the opportunity to see what is going on in the mind and body as we imagine relationships with others.

Bringing mindfulness to what is going on in the body and the mind when we imagine someone we care for, helps us to be more aware of the feelings we have in relationships that nurture us. Remembering them may trigger feelings of joy or sadness. Remembering them may bring a deep sense of gratitude or even the warmth of a selfless wish for their wellbeing. Whatever comes, this helps us to be more aware of the kind of feelings that are the lifeblood of our being and reminds us how important they are in our lives.

When we imagine someone we do not know, we start to create a story about them. We begin to relate to them through the story in our minds. This gives us a window through which we may see how we piece fragments of information together to create an idea of a person and what is going on in their lives. We may even see how our ideas about this person are shaped by our preconceptions, stereotypes and prejudices.

We become author and audience of a story in the mind in which we play a cameo role. As we imagine the characters in this play, we create relationships with them. How do we feel about these characters? Do these feelings change as they come alive in the story we create in the mind?

In the third scenario, we imagine a situation that brings up uncomfortable feelings. **Do not bring to mind a traumatic event outside of a supportive social context of therapy, an experienced mindfulness meditation teacher or well-established group of experienced meditators where you feel safe.** Likewise, if you are going through a difficult time of change or grief and are relatively new to mindfulness meditation, do not to follow this section of this guided mindfulness practice as this may make things worse.

Imagining situations that produce difficult feelings in the controlled environment of meditation gives us the opportunity to become more aware of the feelings themselves and how they can make us think and react. This helps us shift our reaction from an avoidance response to the uncomfortable sensory nature of reactive emotions and become curious about what is going on in exactly the same way as the **stretching and sitting** meditation.

The avoidance response produces a sense of threat. We create a narrative that perceives a person as a source of threat and a sense of self that is threatened. If we are just trying to escape experiencing uncomfortable feelings, we may be feeding patterns of denial and burying something we need to process. It is important to just acknowledge feelings that are present and be curious about them.

Being curious about our feelings and thoughts, and what is going on in the lives of those who trigger our emotional reactions, defuses the avoidance response and disengages attention from the narrative that creates a personal story of blame. This helps us to let go feelings of anger, blame and self-criticism as wells as the narrative in which we play the role of victim. Only then can we see things from different perspectives.

Becoming more aware of patterns of thoughts and feelings that come up in difficult relationships helps us to manage them better. Being able to regulate emotions in real life enables us to think more carefully about what the best thing to do might be. Often the best thing to do is nothing – at least until we can speak or act with a clear head and less emotion.

Mindfulness practice enables us to be more aware of the sensory feelings that come with emotions. This helps us to regulate our emotions and not get so caught up in a personal story. This can help us to be calm when we need to speak about things that could create a sense of threat to others and provoke them to reject what we have to say. If we are able to regulate our emotions and be aware of our feelings, we can be more sensitive to how others feel and so make them feel safe and heard, making it easier for them to listen and see things objectively.

There are times, however, where we need to express passion to be authentic. Then we need to be fully aware of our feelings to say what we wish to say in a way that stirs others to follow our lead.

Deepening mindfulness meditation with concentration and allowing the mind to wander

Living in an uncertain world

We are always creating a story out of our imagination. Everything is created out of memories of sensations, feelings and situations mingled with old stories. When we are stressed, we are more likely to interpret what is going on as a potential threat. A sense of threat creates the need to identify the source of the threat. We also imagine who it is that is being threatened. This becomes a sense of self that we feel we need to protect.

Who we believe we are becomes inseparable from the way we see things. When the way we see things is challenged by others, we take things personally. The greater the sense of threat, the more our senses are tuned to perceive its source and the mind works to devise a strategy to counter it. We can fail to take in new information and can get trapped by our preconceptions. We fail to consider the facts and end up being driven by our biases. We do not hear information that does not conform to our views. We make bad decisions. We fail to listen to others making them feel ignored and disempowered.

Mindfulness practice increases body-based awareness, reduces stress and disperses the defensive self-creations of the mind. This enables physiological processes to function as they are supposed to – at baseline levels that we would normally feel if we felt safe and connected to others around us.

It is only possible to perceive new information and be curious about it when we feel safe. If we can apply mindfulness in an uncertain world to remain curious, we can respond creatively to change. Learning to 'drop the story' breaks down a separate sense of self. Connecting with others creates a sense of shared identity, making it possible to work together in the service of the collective good.

Concentration and allowing the mind to wander meditation

The **concentration and allowing the mind to wander** meditation involves:

1. Concentrating on sensations of breathing to calm the mind and body;
2. Holding an upright and awake posture-grounding awareness in the body;
3. Allowing the mind to wander; and
4. When you become aware your attention has become distracted, bringing awareness back to the body by checking and adjusting posture if necessary.

How many times have you lost your keys and searched for them with a sense of frustration? Sooner or later you give up. Then perhaps you make a cup of tea and sit down for a moment or you do something else and put solving the problem of the lost keys on hold for a while. Then, when the sense of frustration has lifted, your mind somehow starts to work. Your body leads you to your lost keys or maybe you just see them because your perception is no longer impaired by stress and you can now notice things around you. Maybe you just remember where you put them. Often answers come by not doing anything at all. The **concentration and allowing the mind to wander** meditation works in a similar way.

This meditation is a short form of what becomes the main mindfulness meditation practice. It starts with sitting upright and focusing attention on sensations of breathing, which calms the body and produces clarity of awareness. When the mind has settled, it becomes possible to relax the effort of focusing attention on sensations of breathing. Awareness remains grounded in feelings in the body. Sensations of breathing rise and fall. Attention forms around objects of thought, sound and sensations and then dissolves into a field of awareness grounded in the body, as they fade in awareness.

Up until this stage in the programme all the meditation practices have involved concentration: focussing attention on body-based sensations, see Figure 3a. When the mind wanders, the task is to return attention to that object. The first stage of the **concentration and allowing the mind to wander** meditation is a form of 'concentration meditation' that uses the breath as the object of concentration in a similar way to the **posture and breath** meditation, see Figure 3a.

The second stage in the **concentration and allowing the mind to wander** meditation is 'open monitoring', see Figure 3b. Concentration meditation reduces mental activity and open monitoring meditation allows conscious mind-wandering in a relaxed state, which may have some similar effects to dreaming. Over time this releases deeper patterns imprinted on the mind and body.

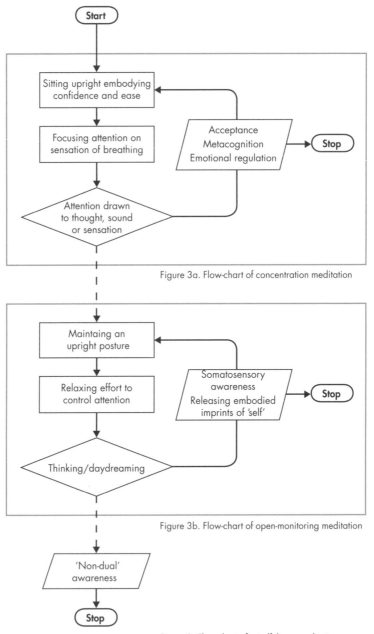

Figure 3a. Flow-chart of concentration meditation

Figure 3b. Flow-chart of open-monitoring meditation

Figure 3. Flow-chart of mindfulness meditation

Epilogue

The path of no return

Have you ever seen a trout jump? The trout's reaction is triggered by a fleeting sight of an insect or glint of light reflected by small-fry. There's a splash. When there is no wind, hatching aquatic insect larvae get trapped by the surface tension of the water and are easy prey. Then trout can be seen swimming leisurely 'sipping' flies trapped in the surface film of the water of the lake.

Sometimes trout are feeding a little deeper, taking larvae swimming from the bottom of a lake to hatch. Then trout do not break the surface at all but sometimes it is possible to see a 'boil' on the surface as the fish swim up from below and quickly turn to take an insect larva. Sometimes trout are feeding in the depths or just lying low and nothing stirs on the surface of the lake.

Thoughts are like trout jumping in a lake. Patterns of feelings created by imprints of past experiences are like movements of water produced by the wind. These invisible currents concentrate insect larvae in different places in the lake and this is where you will find the trout. They rise to take larvae, like attention forming around thoughts arising in the mind. The water is like the awareness in which everything arises in experience.

The rationale in Mindfulness-Based Cognitive Therapy (MBCT) is cognitive. It is based on a psychological understanding of the way people get depressed. Mindfulness helps people who are at risk of depression to stop applying problem-solving strategies to low mood, which feed patterns of self-doubt. Instead, just learning to notice what is arising in the mind, accepting it as it is and being curious, changes the way people relate to themselves. It is like watching trout jumping for flies instead of getting frustrated because it is impossible to catch them with your hands.

There is increasing evidence that this approach to mindfulness reduces stress and has a number of benefits to well-being, quality of life and even cognitive performance, however, the Mindfulness-Based Organisational Education (MBOE) programme sees mindfulness differently. It explains how patterns of thoughts, emotions and behaviour are imprinted in the body and how all of this makes us social beings shaped by identity and culture.

Feelings in the body are an expression of subtle emotional changes that become thoughts. As mindfulness meditation practice progresses, awareness becomes increasingly grounded in the body and the problem-solving patterns of the mind become increasingly less intrusive. Now patterns of thinking and feeling become more like trout leisurely sipping hatching larvae caught in the surface film of the lake.

As the mind settles, the meditator becomes aware of subtle feelings that come with thoughts. These subtle feelings are like boils on the surface as trout take larvae below. Now it is possible to focus attention on feelings in the body rather than follow thoughts as they emerge. Then these feelings disperse, and a thought does not even form in the mind.

In time, it is possible to sit and little arises. Feelings in the body become still and little moves in the depths of the body. This is like fish swimming slowly, deep below the surface of the lake. The sense of subject and object becomes increasingly indistinct as the mind becomes absorbed in undifferentiated, 'non-dual' awareness, see Figure 3.

But sustaining this level of stillness in the mind takes more than merely watching the mind and grounding awareness in the body. This is only possible when we can clearly see that the separate sense of self is an illusion and we wish to be free from the suffering it causes us. The separate sense of self will not give way, however, until we can dissolve any sense of threat from others with a sense of universal relatedness. This comes slowly as we develop our understanding of the human condition and can feel compassion for human suffering in all its forms.

This is why developing the ability to rest the mind in a 'non-dual' state, insight into the illusion of the separate self and proso-cial motivation are three facets of the same thing. They produce an authentic leader who can create trust because others recognise she will prioritises interests of the group over and above her own.

Enlightenment

So long as the sense of self is shaped by patterns of thinking and behaviour designed to protect its interests over and above those of others, it will leave a shadow. It will fear loss and rejection and these fears will shape patterns of brain connectivity and leave physiolog-ical imprints on the body.

When we learn to value embodied feelings that come with kindness and understanding more than a narrative of self and other, all goes well. We can feel disoriented when we realise that the per-son we believe ourselves to be, is a construction of the mind. How this changes our sense of self can produce overwhelming experi-ences as nervous connections change and the embodied imprints of past patterns are released.

In Christian contemplative traditions, these experiences are described as the Dark Night of the Soul. They are the kind of experiences the Buddha is said to have had in his encounter with Mara, the Lord of Death, meditating under the Bodhi Tree before his enlightenment. For some, these types of experience can trigger psychotic reactions, which can have serious long-term effects.

When we realise this imaginary being is no longer useful to us, we fear its end. We grasp at anything that gives it reason to exist.

When the rational mind has been trained to repress emotions or the sense of self has been shaped through traumatic or socially disconnected conditions, the imprint of our imaginations will be deep and there may be a struggle when they collapse. Having glimpsed the insubstantial nature of our constructions, we may confuse our fantasies with reality. This process needs to be managed carefully.

Traditional use of psychotropic drugs (entheogens) or physical trials in rituals can have powerful transformative effects, however, they come with a psychological risk if they take place outside a traditional cultural context in which the individual is embedded. Mindfulness offers a more gradual and safe approach as it can be understood rationally. It does not depend on magical power.

Even with mindfulness, however, processing imprints of the separate self can still be disturbing if awareness is not grounded in the body and the process takes place in the absence of a supportive social setting. Dedicating trials experienced on The Path and its fruit to the greater good ensures progress and protects the traveller on their journey.

The body and the nervous system may take years to process what is taking place. This is why it is important to establish supportive social and emotional connections. It is always best to take things one step at a time, rather than strive for transformation through intensive practice.

The object of mindfulness practice is not to become super-human. It is to become more human. This is because it helps us to become more self-aware and respond with kindness to our own needs and those of others.

Humans always believe in some mythological source of power, which binds them together. Hierarchical leaders divide and rule. We are ready to swallow lies to protect what we value. We do everything we can to maintain the spell that gives us a sense of identity. Waking up is a risky business. Speaking out will provoke a reaction.

Today, the promise of self-improvement drives the economy, however, inequality has to be managed to maintain stability.

We are entering times, where opportunity for self-improvement is shrinking and there is an increasing gulf between the powerful and the disempowered. There is a growing risk of unrest and no-one is in control.

The autonomy, competence and relatedness, which is the fruit of social mindfulness, creates a new narrative. Insight, awareness and compassion become ideals of leadership that bring people together to build a resilient culture, see Figure 4.

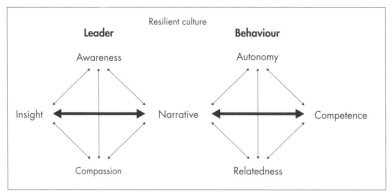

Figure 4. Leadership mindfulness

Social mindfulness gives us the intrinsic rewards of feelings unconflicted by thinking and action. The illusion of zero-sum–individualistic gain, loses its power to control. We understand how to shape a world of possibility with intention, for the good of all.

Glossary

Approach/Avoidance

modes are responses to an object, sensation or thought. An important aspect of **mindfulness practice** involves applying curiosity to uncomfortable **feelings** to reduce patterns of avoidance.

Attention

may be focused on any object that comes into **awareness,** including sensations, **feelings**, thoughts, ideas, stories, ourselves, others or activities.

Awareness

always comes with an object of **awareness** i.e. sensations, **feelings**, thoughts, people, ideas etc. **Mindfulness meditation** develops awareness of body-based feelings with a sense of safety and relatively low levels of mental activity. With **mindfulness practice**, body-based **feelings** become a 'field of **awareness**' in which particular sensations, **feelings** and thoughts arise. Then, **feelings** in the 'field of **awareness**' change as particular sensations, **feelings** and thoughts arise. Noticing changes in this 'field of **awareness**' is the felt aspect of **metacognition.**

Body-based awareness

is produced by perception of stimulation of nerve endings in the skin, **fascia,** muscles and viscera. These include **proprioception, interoception** and **soma-tosensory perception.**

Default Mode Network (DMN)

is the network of connections in the brain responsible for human **higher cogni-tive functions.** Under chronic conditions of perceived social threat, the **DMN** is responsible for producing the internal narrative of self-criticism and blame. The **DMN** is also responsible for **problem-solving** and, under conditions of socially constructed safety, insight and creativity. Focusing **attention** on any object or activity interrupts mind-wandering produced by the **DMN**. From a neurological perspective, the object of **mindfulness practice** is to establish a reduced level of activity of mind-wandering produced by the **DMN** under an experiential state free from socially constructed threat i.e. a state of social safety. This is a state of receptive **awareness** of body-based **feelings** and creative patterns of thinking, which produce insight and prosocial, playful behaviour.

Discrepancy monitoring

is the function of comparing current conditions of experience with an imagined set of conditions. This is important in **problem-solving** but 'wanting things to be different to the way they are' or, more positively, feeling relieved that things are not as bad as they might be, can have range of negative effects. This can interfere with focus, produce negative cognitive bias, block feelings, undermine confidence, cause stress etc. **Mindfulness practice** involves selectively learning to disengage **discrepancy monitoring** by applying curiosity to trigger the **approach mode**.

Emotions

are the subjective experience of different states of physiological arousal that prepare and animal to do what it needs to do to survive. Emotional states are triggered by internal signals that regulate feeding, rest, reproduction and /or environmental triggers for example fight-or-flight reactions to threat. Generally, animal emotions are state changes that are short-lived or sustained so long as the survival related behaviour produced by the physiological state continues.

Fascia

are thin layers of connective tissue that hold soft tissues in place. **Fascia** also act as a diffuse vascular system for lymph. Fascial function is impaired by stress hormones, poor **posture** and sedentary lifestyles, which lead to stiffness, musculoskeletal damage and pain.

Feelings

can be sensory perceptions of body-based sensations, which may be produced by changes in arousal states (raw **emotions**) e.g. 'butterflies in the belly', OR subjective states produced by interactions between patterns of thinking and raw **emotions** e.g. envy, love etc. Unlike raw **emotions**, however, these complex **feelings** can be maintained over long periods of time and can be triggered by thinking and or **feelings** that trigger patterns of thinking.

Higher cognitive functions

of the human mind evolved to enable individuals to navigate relationships and changing roles in complex, dynamic social environments. We have the most advanced ability to construct mental models of processes and ideas about the world, including ourselves and others, of any other animal. The neurological correlative of **higher cognitive function** is the **default mode network**. In contemporary society we often assume that thinking functions independently from **feelings** and **emotion**.

Interoception

is the perception of sensations in the viscera (heart, lungs and gut) via the **vagus nerve**.

Metacognition

or **metacognitive awareness** is the ability to perceive thoughts and thinking as objects and processes as well as recognise that they are ideas about things and not the things themselves. In **mindfulness meditation**, **metacognition** may also include awareness of sensations, emotional states and **feelings** as objects of **awareness**. **Metacognition** is applying the ability we have to imagine what is going through another's mind (*Theory of Mind*) to our own mind.

Mindfulness

or 'mindful' is often used in vague and ill-defined ways. As the benefits of **mindfulness practice** are due to restoration of the ability to disengage the **DFM** at proper times, **mindfulness** is no more than cognitive functioning free from chronic stress. Defining **mindfulness** as a psychological trait is only likely to be relevant in a society where there are high rates of chronic stress. **Mindfulness** may, therefore, appear to be a state that is untroubled by stress. The danger of defining **mindfulness** as a state or trait, therefore, is that it may become understood as a positive, non-reactive or passive mind-state of present-moment awareness, which is characterised by an absence of critical thinking and purposeful action.

Mindfulness meditation

is an attentional training, which involves focusing **attention** on a chosen sensory object (or maintain **awareness** grounded in body-based **feelings**) and noticing the way **attention** is drawn to thoughts or sense perceptions that come into **awareness**. **Mindfulness meditation** develops the capacity to disengage the **DFM** at proper times and so engage different cognitive functions appropriately.

Mindfulness practice

includes formal **mindfulness meditation** and informal **mindfulness** exercises practiced during the day e.g. paying **attention** to sensations in the skin while having a shower and noticing the way **attention** is drawn to thoughts and how the mind wanders.

Mindfulness meditation

develops the capacity to disengage the **DFM** at proper times and so engage different cognitive functions appropriately.

Overgeneralised memory

over-applies the human mind's capacity to make generalisations about past events and is associated with depression. It may be linked to the way people discount information that challenges their perspective. As **mindfulness practice** involves developing the capacity to notice what is taking place from moment-to-moment (**metacognitive awareness**), new observations are likely to challenge fixed perspectives. Developing **specific memory** acts as a corrective and is only possible if **attention** is monitoring moment-to-moment experience i.e. **specific memory** and **mindfulness** are two sides of the same coin. **Awareness** of present-moment conditions is only possible by noticing and comparing current sensory inputs with those which have taken place in previous moments. Memory and **awareness** are closely connected.

Posture

in social animals communicates social status. Stress from socially produced sense of anxiety affects thinking, mood and posture. Adopting better posture can have a positive effect on **feelings**/mood, cognitive function, social behaviour and relationships.

Problem-solving

is a defining characteristic of the **higher cognitive functions** of the human mind, however, it is a 'two-edged sword'. It comes with an implicit sense of threat and requires the abstract construction of individuals, objects and relationships of causal action, which easily become the building blocks of zero-sum game frameworks of reference. Clearly, objectification, definition and measurement are required to understand and manipulate mechanisms, however, this can be unhelpful in understanding and navigating complex interactive systems and produce social/emotional disconnection. Over **problem-solving** is also implicated as a cause of poor resilience and stress. Today, social status is closely linked to ability to 'solve problems'. Fusing **problem-solving** with a socially constructed sense of self results in drive to improve social status and this leads to the creation of hierarchical social structures. In depressions, **problem-solving** becomes pathological as it directed at the self-construct of the individual who applies it to their own subjective experience.

Proprioception

is the sensory system that informs the brain about body **posture** and movement. This sensory system relays signals from nerve endings that are triggered by stretching **fascia** and muscles.

Relatedness

is a sense of connection with others and of common humanity. **Relatedness** is fundamental to what it means to be human.

Social baseline theory (SBT)

explains why we feel safe and content in a group. Herd animals feel safe in a group because there are many eyes and ears that can detect a predator. Humans, however, have a highly developed sense of self. When we feel anxious about our place in the world, the **higher cognitive functions** of the human mind actively create a narrative that defines self and the source of threat as other. When we feel safe in a relationship or group, there is less activity in **DFM**, and we lose the sense of a separate self. We share our sense of identify with a partner or the group in which we feel safe. **Mindfulness practice** has a similar effect. The effect of feeling safe in a group and **mindfulness practice**, not only reduce emotional distress but also reduce the level of activation in regions in the brain that respond to pain from physical injury or disease.

Social mindfulness

combines mindfulness practice with **relatedness**. This develops insight into the way we construct a separate sense of self in conditions of threat and how this produces stress, self-serving behaviour and social disconnection. Increased **awareness** of body-based **feelings** combined with **relatedness** and insight into the way we create a sense of self, reduces self-critical thinking, blame, bias based on stereotypes and increases the capacity for understanding, compassion, critical analysis and prosocial action. **SBT** explains how humans are adapted to live in safe social environment. **Mindfulness practice** acts as a corrective to maladapted **DMN** function produced by chronic states of socially constructed threat.

Social mindfulness

combines mindfulness practice with **relatedness**. This develops insight into the way we construct a separate sense of self in conditions of threat and how this produces stress, self-serving behaviour and social disconnection. Increased **awareness** of body-based **feelings** combined with insight into the way we create a sense that creates a sense of **relatedness**, reduces self-critical thinking, blame, bias based on stereotypes and increases the capacity for understanding, compassion, critical analysis and prosocial action. **SBT** explains how humans are adapted to live in safe social environment. **Mindfulness practice** acts as a corrective to maladapted **DMN** function produced by chronic states of socially constructed threat.

Somatosensory

perception is the perception of **feelings** in the body. This may include **interoception** of sensations in the viscera via the **vagus nerve** but also includes sensations of pain, pressure, temperature etc. produced by nerve endings in the skin muscles, joints and **fascia**.

Specific memory

is the capacity to recall specific details about events and experience. Developing **specific memory** capacity plays a part in cognitive therapy as it can be used to record observations about experience that may then be compared with overgeneralised memories. **Specific memory** is developed in **mindfulness** programmes by recollecting specific details of experience noticed during **mindfulness practice**. **Specific memory** and **mindfulness** enable a person to separate witnessed observation from **feelings**. This reduces bias, and improves communication and the capacity to learn from experience.

The vagus nerve

has an evolutionary ancient origin and transmits **feelings** slowly to the brain. This is because the part of the nerve, which is responsible for transmitting sensations to the brain is unmyelinated. An example of a feeling transmitted to the brain via the **vagus nerve** is "butterflies" produced nerve endings in the gut.

Vagal tone

is a measure of overall physiological health that is based on a measure of heart rate variability entrained with breathing. Heart rate slows on the out-breath with a physiological calming response triggered by parasympathetic activation. Heart rate increases on the in-breath triggered by sympathetic activation. Increasing the relative duration of the out-breath to the in-breath will reduce the overall heart rate and so reduce the level of stress.